Corfu Sketches

A thirty-year journey

Sketches by Theresa Nicholas   Text by John Waller

HARBOUR 1961

"I think no place on Earth can be lovelier than this"

Edward Lear

22nd February 1856

There was an Old Man of Corfu
who never knew what he should do;
So he rushed up and down
till the sun made him brown,
That bewildered Old Man of Corfu

Acknowledgements

I thank Louise Etherington for her support, Rob Kesseler on the design of the book, Agalis Manessis for her comments on all things Corfiot, Hilary Whitton Paipeti for her knowledge of the villages, Jim Potts on the poetry and Bill and Barbara Pope for the maps.

CORFU SKETCHES Copyright © 2008
Sketches by Theresa Nicholas, text by John Waller

Published in 2008 by **YIANNIS BOOKS**
101 Strawberry Vale, Twickenham, TW1 4SJ, UK
Tel. 0044 2088923433

Typesetting and layout by Mike Cooper, 25 Orchard Rd, Sutton SM1 2QA
Printed by Antony Rowe, Chippenham, Wiltshire

www.yiannisbooks.com

128pp
ISBN 978-0-9547887-4-2

Contents

To the Mayor of Corfu

Κερκυρα, Κερκυρα, το πρασινο νησι!
Ποιος θα βρει την λυση
Να προστατεψουμε την φυση;
        —Εμεις, ολοι μας , μαζι!

Kerkyra, Kerkyra, to prasino nisi!
Poios tha vrei tin lisi
Na prostatepsoume tin fisi?
        Emeis, oloi mas mazi!

Corfu, Corfu, the green island
Who will find the solution
And protect nature?
        We will, all of us together!

Jim Potts

My wife and I fell in love with your island in 1966. In 1971 we built a little summer house on a deserted mountainside above the wild west coast. Throughout the 1970s we explored the island with family and Greek friends. The 1980s brought mass tourism to Corfu and, like many others, our love waned.

Over the last few years, many positive initiatives have given us hope for the future: villages such as Benitses, wrecked by lager-louts, have been reborn; the olive groves are no longer being cut down for firewood for Italian pizza ovens; the Corfu Trail now stretches the length of the island and Corfiots are being trained up as guides for the walks.

Improvements to Corfu Town started with the European summit in 1994 and have led to its recognition this year as a World Heritage Site.

The 2007 Symposium '*Cleaning up the Mediterranean*', organised by the Durrell School of Corfu and the DDIKEOMA Institute, asked you to turn the green island of Corfu into the 'greenest' in the Mediterranean, thereby encouraging eco-tourism to the island, by:

- preserving the island's EU Natura 2000 conservation sites, in particular the Lagoons of Korission and Antionoti;
- implementing a full scale recycling programme;
- encouraging the use of alternative energy;
- supporting the setting up of a Marine Reserve between the Diapontian Islands;
- encouraging the compliance by local organisations with ISO's Environmental Management Systems standards; and
- introducing a park-and-ride scheme.

Theresa's sketches will bring home to you the architectural treasures in the town and the villages. We ask you to value them and ensure that development does not destroy them.

Theresa Nicholas – the Observer of Corfu

By Jim Potts

Theresa first came to Corfu in 1961. If Corfu has an observer of its folklore and old customs equivalent to Dorset's Thomas Hardy, then Theresa Nicholas surely qualifies.

In her art she has recorded Corfiot life as she knew it from the early days, as it used to be lived: old olive-presses, village life, women with donkeys and mules, wine cellars, buildings and architectural features, churches and belfries, chimneys, costumes and interesting characters, all sorts of fascinating old images, man-made and natural, captured before they (largely) disappeared. Theresa has followed her eye and in consequence has witnessed aspects of life in Corfu that few foreigners have been privileged to see.

She started illustrating Corfu scenes soon after she arrived, but much of her work was commercial. 'I churned them out for tourists', she admits. But they gave her a means of survival until 1980, when she started doing more serious work, experimenting with mixed media compositions, as well as linocuts, woodcuts, monoprints, etchings and oil-paintings.

She has exhibited in Corfu, in 1996, 2002 and 2004.

Theresa has been a great walker in her day. She tells that in the early days peasants were amazed at the sight of foreigners walking: *'Me ta podhia? Dhen echeis aftokinito?'* (You're going on foot? Don't you have a car?)

Her home and small studio near Kanoni is a true artist's garret, and it is fascinating to see her precious works, which she is reluctant to sell, hanging from every wall.

We are now lucky that we can buy copies of her sketches. Corfu does not know what an artist it has in its midst.

Jim Potts OBE worked for the British Council from 1969, in Ethiopia, Kenya, Greece, the UK, and – as British Council Director – in Czechoslovakia, Australia and Sweden. He lives in Corfu and is the author of *Corfu Blues*. This article appeared in the *Corfiot* in June 2006.

Using this book

This is not just a coffee-table book.

Please take it with you when you travel into town or drive through the countryside. Use it as a guide. See your journey through an artist's eyes. Perhaps pick up a few snippets of information from me.

Let's first go to Corfu town. Turn to page 17, which shows five walks around the World Heritage Site. To help you choose your route, I have selected some of Theresa's water-colour sketches – these appear on the following pages. I then show, for each walk, a more detailed map followed by a number of pen and ink sketches.

Follow the map on the detailed section of the walk. In town, stop looking at the shops. Look up: see the faces on the keystones; admire the ornamented doors; even check out the chimneys, though this can be difficult as the routes you take are often through narrow alleyways.

Ignore the window fronts in the tourist and shopping areas which have tried to change the character of the town;

behind the façade, the heart of the town is still the same. Come late in the evening or early on Sunday morning before the tourists arrive; you could be walking through a medieval town.

It is now time to visit the secrets of Corfu. Leave the main roads and discover some of the 104 villages that hide in the interior of the island. Some are active, others are derelict; but all are beautiful.

Leave your car at the entrance to the village and walk through its lanes, admiring the unique architecture – the *botzo*, the access balcony, and enjoy the faded colours. We are not in Aegean Greece with its blue doors and white walls; we are in Ionian Greece with its green woodwork and Venetian red walls. Look at the old iron gates and the bell towers – they are all different.

During the day, visit the mini-market to buy your picnic and, best of all, your fresh locally-baked bread. In the evening, go into the village grill room for your take-away *giros*: pork, onion, tomato and *tsatsiki* all wrapped in a *pita* bread. Or linger longer and choose something off the *souvli*, the rotating spit, or cooked just for you over the charcoal fire. Perhaps, on your way home, after you have watched the sun go down, stop off at the local taverna.

Now turn to page 64 and choose which villages you will visit. They are clustered in the old regions of the island, the Messis near the town, the Gyro in the north-west of the island and the Oros, in the north-east. Run through the sketches and find your favourites and then check which region they are in. Then go to the details for each region and read about each village. Theresa did not sketch in the southern region of Lefkimmi, but there are many fine villages to find there as well.

Finally, before visiting a village, turn to page 109 and glance at Theresa's sketches of village life. Over the last few years, much has changed. Work in the summer is now in the tourist industry not in the fields or the olive groves; the olives are harvested over the winter. Some of the sights are still there but you need to look hard to find them.

The characters portrayed are still to be found if you pop into the village *cafenion* and meet the men. Look into the houses as you pass, and sure enough you will see the faces of the women that Theresa drew.

Come and join us on our trip. *Kalo taxidi*, good journey.

Corfu

World Heritage Site

"Overall, the Old Town of Corfu is a unique cultural entity of a high aesthetic value:

- The aesthetic value it encompasses is recognised in the structure and form of the town, as well as its arts, letters and social life.
- The Old Town developed over time, through the gradual assimilation of features of the two worlds on the Mediterranean, the East and West.
- It has been preserved, alive and substantially unaltered, until the present day."

Nomination for inclusion on the UNESCO World Heritage List Accepted June 29, 2007

Corfu – World Heritage Site

In 1848, Edward Lear, famous for being the inventor of the 'Limerick' but actually of greater importance as the most talented topographical painter of his generation, in *Corfu Years*, wrote:

> "We anchored in the beautiful paradise of Corfu bay … The city was Venetian until 1780, but has little to recommend it – narrow streets and poky houses. But nearest the sea, there is the most beautiful esplanade in the world. On the further side of this is the magnificent Palace of the Viceroy and beyond is the double-crowned Citadel – very picturesque."

Time moves on and tastes change. In 1937, Lawrence Durrell, in *Prospero's Cell*, wrote:

> "The architecture of the town is Venetian; the houses above the old port are built up elegantly into slim tiers with narrow alleys and colonnades running between them; red, yellow, pink, umber – a jumble of pastel shades which the moonlight transforms into a dazzling white city built for a wedding cake."

His younger brother, Gerald Durrell, in *My Family and Other Animals*, wrote:

> "Around us the town rose steeply, tiers of multi-coloured houses piled haphazardly, green shutters folded back from the windows like the wings of a thousand moths."

In 1966, my version, in *Greek Walls*, was less poetic but just as emotional:

> "Then out of the haze, slowly, magically, appeared Corfu Town with her magnificent buildings between two enormous forts. It was love at first sight."

For cruise ship passengers, I hope it will also be love at first sight. For those that fly in and eventually come to town, I ask you not to despair about the car parking, but to make your way to Edward Lear's most beautiful esplanade in the world and wander the streets of the Old Town. I am sure you will understand why it is now a World Heritage Site.

Attending the Planning Committee of the London Borough of Richmond I learnt the meaning of the words: 'Townscape importance'.

Simply put, a city street built, say, in the 1890s would be architecturally important if the great majority of the houses were original, but would lose its importance once a certain percentage had been changed or replaced. None of the buildings would be worthy of listing, but the whole ensemble would earn its merit by its 'townscape'. Corfu is like this.

The Old Town has a handful of gorgeous buildings: the Town Hall built by the Venetians between 1683 and 1691; the Liston, built by the French after 1807; and the Palace of St. Michael and St. George, built by the British between 1814 and 1824.

The real beauty of the architecture is the almost total absence of modern building amongst the centuries of Venetian construction. Much of it is at least four-storeys high, often built on narrow streets. Space was at a premium; this was an early example of high-density living. Indeed, one of the selling points in the nomination for inclusion of the Old Town in the World Historic List is the presence of the first 'flat-dwellers' in Greece.

Along the alleys, one can walk today as if having arrived in a time-capsule. Wander off the Tourist Trail; your journey will be safe and spell-binding.

The Venetian presence on Corfu created the town we love. How did this corner of the Byzantine Empire fall under the sway of Venice? In 1204, the Fourth Crusade, led by the 80-year old Doge of Venice Enrico Dandolo, rather than recapture Jerusalem, ransacked Constantinople and divided up the Empire. As John Julius Norwich, in *Byzantium*, wrote: "It was Constantinople's darkest hour

– even darker, perhaps, than that, two and a half centuries later, which was to see the city's final fall to the Ottoman Sultan."

Campielo

Venice was rewarded for its dastardly deed by receiving the Ionian Islands as its share of the booty. Within sixty-five years, Charles of Anjou had obtained Corfu and the Angevin occupation started. Charles tried to replace the Orthodox Church by the Catholic one but failed. Corfu was divided into four regions whose names are still known today, and are used later in the book when we look at the villages.

The inhabitants of the Old Fort were driven out and moved into what is now the historic centre. Finally, and perhaps most significantly, during this period the Jews were expelled from Spain and settled in the area of the old town known as the Campielo. Walk through it today and you are re-living over 700 years of history.

On May 20th 1386 the Council of Corfu asked Venice for protection and four hundred years of Venetian rule started. Corfu lies at the entrance to the Adriatic Sea and on the route to Venice itself. It was therefore in Venice's interest to build up the fortifications of the Old Fort in the 15thC, and then construct the New Fort and a city wall to the west at the end of the 16thC. The success in doing so, with a little help from the patron saint Agios Spiridon whose relics arrived in Corfu from Constantinople soon after its final fall, kept the Turks at bay on a number of occasions.

case for thanking the Venetians is enhanced when we consider the island itself, with its three million olive trees and 104 villages.

The Venetian lion on the New Fort's main gate

In the successful submission for inclusion in UNESCO's World Heritage List, the two forts and the mainly Venetian historic centre were highlighted. Perhaps the black clouds of the fall of Constantinople in 1204 and 1453 had a silver lining: the Venetians and the arrival of Agios Spiridon. The

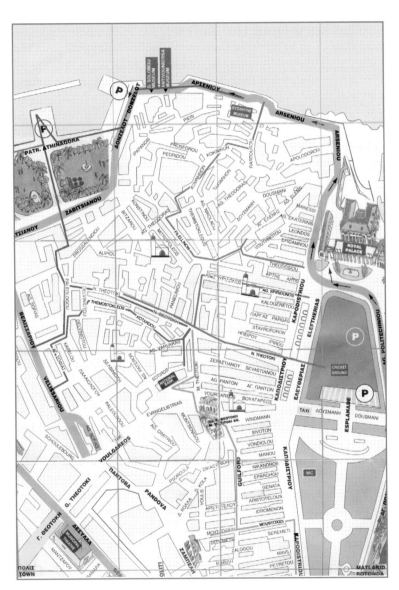

Choose your walk in town:

———— **The Tourist Trail** (Page 33)

The introduction to the World Heritage site takes you from the Cricket Ground through the arches, the Liston, where everyone meets, along the main tourist street and back via the church of Agios Spyridon, Corfu's patron saint.

———— **Through the Old Town** (Page 39)

My favourite walk from the Liston gives you a chance to wander through narrow alleys, where people have lived for over 700 years, via beautiful squares to the Mourayia, the sea walls that defended the town, and the Byzantine Museum.

———— **To the Jewish Quarter** (Page 42)

Leave the centre of the Tourist Trail, shown on the front cover, and tread streets rarely visited by tourists to finish in an area much-changed but still housing the restored synagogue. Artisans used to work here before the days of mass-production.

———— **Via the Old Port and market** (Page 51)

From the centre again, go to the Old Port and market. The sketches show it as it was in the 1960s.

———— **To the smart end of town** (Page 55)

From the centre again, make your way through the gorgeous Old Town Hall Square and up the hill past antique shops and elegant tavernas to where Gerald Durrell first stayed in 1935.

Use the maps of the walks at the start of each section on the page numbers indicated above. To help you choose your walk, see the sketches on the following pages.

Along the Tourist Trail . . .

The Old Fort

Built by the Venetians in 15th C. Go through this entrance and climb to the top. What a view of the town, the island and over to Albania!

The Square of the Saint

In the centre is now a statue of George Theotokis, Prime Minister of Greece in the 19th C. Ahead is the 16th C Church of Agios Spiridon, the island's patron saint. To the right is the 17th C Church of the Blessed Virgin of Strangers and behind you is the 16th C Church of John the Baptist.

ΚΑΠΝΟΠΟΛΕΙΟΝ "ΜΙΝΙΟΝ"
ΝΙΚ. ΑΓΑΘΟΣ
TOBACCONIST "MIGNON"
NIKO.. AGATHOS

THE HOUSE of DANIEL GOBIS 1680

THE PINA PINECONE

THE PINA

Nikiforou Theotoki Street, the main tourist street. All other walks can start from here. Nikiforos Theotokis was the great scientist and Archbishop of Astrakhan and Stavropol in 18thC.

The tobacconist and greengrocer still exist. The pinecone has disappeared. Under the arches on the right at No. 47, visit George at M. Tourmougolou for good books.

Through the Old Town . . .

Covered arcades, known in Corfu as *'volta'*, keep you cool in summer and dry in winter.

Doorway of 18 Filellinon Street, opposite the Durrell School of Corfu at No. 11. **Look carefully**; they are pomegranates!

CORFU   TAEKETA NICHOLAS

Ag. Elenis Square

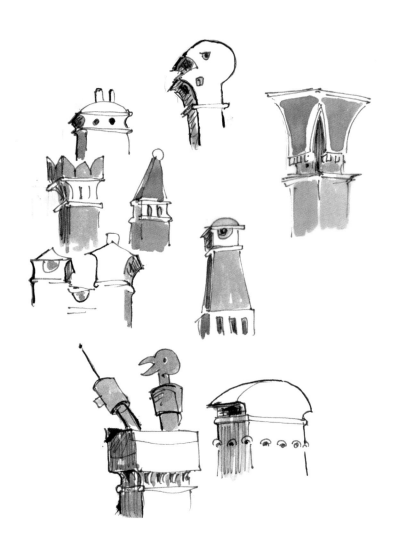

In Ag. Andreas Square, behind Ag. Andreas Church which is on the left of the sketch of the Mourayia (page 23), looking north through the new electricity poles!

Morayia, the sea walls, sketched from the beach near the Faliraki, which is accessed through one of the two remaining of four original gates through the town walls.

To the Jewish Quarter . . .

41 Themostokleos Kotardou Street.

At far end of Themostokleos Kotardou Street looking down towards Nikiforou Theotoki Street.

Don't be shy, look behind the doors.

An ouzerie at No. 71 Taliologou Street'

A fruit and vegetable stall. Buy a tomato or some grapes; what a flavour!
Go to the market (see page 51) for the freshest of all.

The barber's next to No. 80 Taliologou Street, now selling Barbour clothes!

The Synagogue has been fully restored. Behind it is the New Fort and an area badly bombed in 1941.

To the smart end of town . . .

Sketched from behind the National Bank, which has replaced the low
building in the foreground. The old campanile, built in 1390, is all that
remains of the church of the 'Annunciata' Evangalistra.

No. 59 Guilford Street – a hardware store.

No. 6 Guilford Street.

Πασχα – Easter procession . . .

On Good Friday, the churches in town, in funereal
procession, carry the icon of Jesus Christ which has
been taken down from the Cross.

The main procession is accompanied by many of the island's 22 village bands, dressed in colourful uniforms and made up of musicians of all ages. The Old Philharmonic from1840 is in blue and red.

Along the Tourist Trail . . .

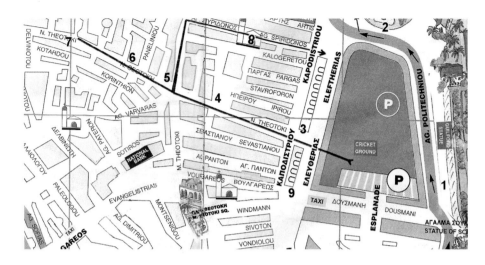

You could easily spend a day on the Tourist Trail: explore the Old Fort and its Museum; visit the exceptional Museum of Oriental Art in the Palace of St. Michael and St. George; shop in the main street of the historic centre; visit the main churches of the town, in particular that of Agios Spiridon, the patron saint of Corfu; and linger long over lunch on the Liston. Or you could spend an hour or two on the Tourist Trail and then venture along the other walks.

Start at the centre of the Cricket ground.

1. To the east is the Old Fort with the Venetian Lion, the view from the south end of the Esplanade (page 34) and the clock tower (page 18).
2. To the north is the British Palace of St. George and St. Michael (page 35).
3. To the west is the Liston built by the French in the style of the Rue de Rivoli (page 35).
4. Pass through the centre of the Liston into Nikiforou Theotoki Street. In 100 metres, on the right is the Square of the Saint (page 18).
5. A further 100 metres on is the centre point of the area (page 19).
6. Above the House of Daniel Cobici on the right are the sculpted heads of the keystones (page 36). Under the arches is the bookshop.
7. Go another 100 metres down Nikiforou Theotoki. See the faces above the building on the left opposite the entrance to Lemonia Square (page 37).
8. Return to the centre point of the area, turn left and then right into Ag. Spiridonas Street and pass the Church of Agios Spiridon (page 38).
9. Finish on the Liston for a cup of coffee. Page 38 shows the corner of the south end of the Liston.

The Venetian Old Fort

In 6thC the Barbarians drove the Corfiots out of their ancient city of Palaiopolis, whose ruins are being excavated south of the town. They settled on the peninsula, whose name Korypho (summit) led to the name Corfu. In 15thC the Venetians built the Old Fort on top of Byzantine walls, and the moat. It withstood the first Turkish siege of 1537, soon after the fall of Constantinople. The Lion of Venice was the symbol of Venetian rule, which lasted from 1386 to 1797.

The view of the Old Fort from the southern end of the Esplanade, the largest town square in the Balkans, made when many of the old houses were demolished to make a free fire area for the canons on the Old Fort. Below the twin 'summits' are the Venetian clock tower (page 18) to the left and, in the foreground, the 19thC English garrison church.

The French Liston

After Napoleon took possession of Corfu in 1797, it came under the protection of Russia and Turkey until 1807, when the French occupied the island until 1814. They built the Liston in the style of the Rue de Rivoli. Today it is where you can meet your friends or wile away time drinking a coffee and reading the paper.

The British Palace and cricket!

From 1814 until 1864 Britain occupied the island, built the Georgian Palace of St. Michael and St. George, drank ginger beer and played cricket. *Tsitsibira* is still made in Corfu. Until the new car park was built, every Wednesday afternoon, *Ow' dat* (Out) would ring out both as the appeal and the umpire's response. *Ochi Sotto* meant not out.

43–49 Nikiforou Theotoki Street

"THE GREEN MAN"

DANIEL · COBICI · MDCLXXX
RINOVATO · DEL 1728

THE SCULPTED HEADS ON THE KEYSTONES OF THE HOUSE OF DANIEL COBICI 1680
RENOVATED 1728

These faces are further down
Niki. Theotoki opposite
entrance to Lemonia Sq

The Church of Agios Spiridon contains, in a silver casket, the remains of the 4thC patron saint of the island which were carried from Constantinople to Corfu in 1453. Miracles ascribed to him include the repulse of the Turkish invasion in 1715.

The southern corner of the Liston.

Through the Old Town . . .

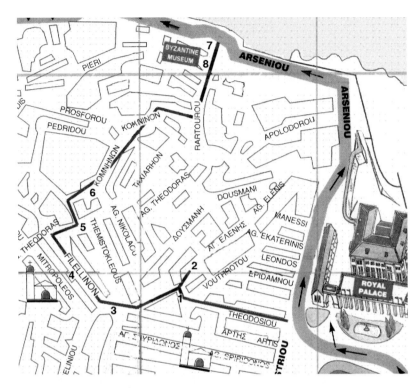

During the Angevin period (1267–1386) overpopulation in the Old Fort forced the residents to move out onto the hill overlooking the Mourayia, the sea walls, in the area now know as the Campielo. At the same time the first Jews arrived, banished from Spain, and settled there too. Today, the multi-storeyed Venetian buildings lining the narrow alleyways, house a vibrant community. To wander through these ancient streets is one of the great pleasures of a visit to the town. Remember, Greece is the safest country in Europe and Corfu is its safest town. If you have time, visit the Byzantine Museum.

Start at the north end of the Liston and take Theodosiou Street, the second after Ag. Spiridonas, into the Old Town.

1. At the end of the street, climb the steps and look back to the left to see the campanile of Ag. Spiridon Church (page 40).
2. At the top on the right is Ag. Elenis Square (page 21).
3. Turn left and walk down Dousmani to the junction with Filellinon on your right. The steps (page 40) are looking up the street.
4. On the right at No. 11 Filellinon is the Durrell School of Corfu and on the left is the doorway of No.18 (page 20).
5. Turn right at end of Filellinon and under the sign to the Venetian Well is the entrance to Kremasti (page 41).
6. The glorious Kremasti Square with the Venetian well in the centre (page 41). Look at the 12 different faces on the well. Leave by the top corner of the square and if lost, don't worry. Aim away from the sun and you will eventually come to the Mourayia, the sea walls.
7. The Mourayia (page 23), sketched from the beach near the Faliraki, which is accessed through only the second of four remaining gates through the old town walls.
8. Behind the church of Ag. Andreas on the left of the sketch of the Mourayia is a square with two electricity poles in the middle. The sketch on page 22 is looking through them from the south!

View of Church of Ag. Spiridon from steps up to Ag. Elenis Square.

View up to Dousmani just below Filellinon.

The entrance to Kremasti Square.

Lino cut of Kremasti Square with the Venetian well in the centre.

To the Jewish Quarter . . .

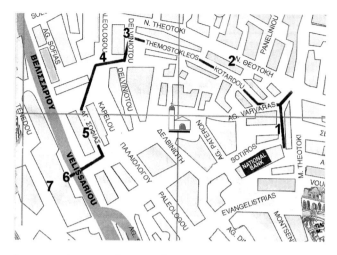

In 1860 the population of Corfu Town was estimated as 17,500, of which one third were Jews. Having been banished from Spain, they had settled in the Old Town during the early 14thC. As well as artisans, they were well respected as the carriers of goods. On 25 April 1944 the German territorial commander, faced with an order to deport the Jewish population from Corfu, insisted that it would cause unrest amongst the Greek population of the town. He then tried to stop the deportations by claiming there was no transport available, that a Red Cross ship in the harbour would fuel 'atrocity propaganda' and that it would lead to 'a loss of ethical prestige in the eyes of the population'. Tragically, in June 1944, 2,000 Jews were deported and only 120 returned. Theresa's sketches are vivid memories of the artisans who worked in the area.

Start in the middle of Nikiforou Theotoki Street (page 19) and pass between the tobacconist and the greengrocer into Ag. Barbara Street.

1. At the end on the left is the Wet Fish Shop with Mr. Fish (page 45) as seen from the shrine to St. Barbara on the right of Ag. Vasiliou, 'Fish Street'. Look up the street (page 43) towards the small square with the replica of the medieval cistern in the centre and back down towards the bottom (page 43). In the 1960s No. 22 was my favourite shop, the Fried Fish Shop (page 44).
2. Do not return to Nikiforou Theotoki Street, but turn left by the shrine into Ag. Barbara Street and immediately right. After 30 metres on your left is No. 41 Themostokleos Kotardou Street (page 24). Between No. 30 and No. 32, look down to the right towards Lemonia Street (page 46). Note No. 13 on the left, with faces on the door and on each corner – to ward off evil spirits?
3. Near the end of Themostokleos Kotardou Street, look down to the right towards Nikiforou Theotoki Street (pages 24 and 46).
4. At the end of the street go down a narrow alley (page 47 left) and look back (page 47 right). Turn left at the bottom into a small square and through an alley at the end into the Jewish Quarter, where Theresa sketched an ouzerie (page 25), a fruit and vegetable stall (page 26), the barber's (page 27), the jewellery shop (page 48) and the tinsmith (page 50).
5. Take the alley to the right into Ag. Sophia Street and on your left is the bell tower of Ag. Sophia, looking south (page 48) and then north (page 49).
6. Finally you come to the view west to the synagogue, which has been restored (page 27).
7. Past the synagogue towards the New Fort is an area with the ruins of houses destroyed by bombing in 1941.

Towards the top of 'Fish Street'.

Towards the bottom of 'Fish Street'.

The Fried Fish Shop

No. 22 Ag. Vasiliou Street.

The Wet Fish Shop.

MR. FISH

The alleyway between 'Fish Steet' and Nikiforou
Theotoki Street.

Between No. 32 and No. 30 Themostikleos
Kotardou Street.

The end of Themostikleos Kotardou Street looking down to
the right.

Looking down the alley at end of
Themostokleos Kotardou Street.

Looking up the alley at end of
Themostokleos Kotardou Street.

The jewellers in the cut-through between Taliologou and Ag. Sophia Streets.

Looking south towards Ag. Sophia bell tower.

street vendor & cart

The Scales

Fish vendor

Looking north towards Ag. Sophia bell tower.

THE COOPER MAKINS
BARRELS WASHTUBS
WASH BOARDS.

In Velissariou Street
opposite the synagogue.

THE JEWISH TINSMITH
SURVIVOR OF THE HOLOCAUST

Next to No. 10 Ag. Sophia Street.

To the Old Port and market . . .

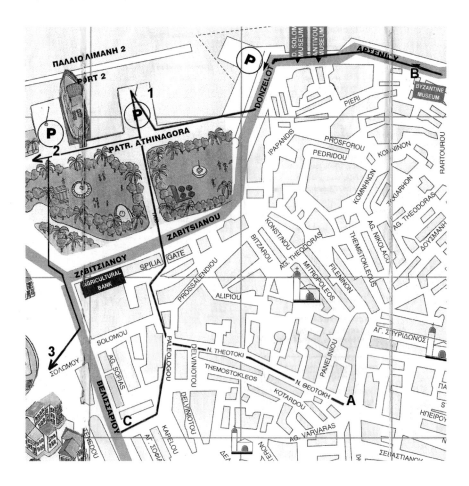

This walk can follow on: (A) from the Tourist Trail by going to the end of Nikiforou Theotoki Street, turning right and through the Spilia Gate; (B) from the Old Town by walking west along the Mourayia, the sea walls; or (C) from the Jewish Quarter by walking north through the Spilia Gate

Much has changed since Theresa made her sketches: the fishing boats are now the ferries to the local islands; the port is a car park and the market has been rebuilt. The New Fort, built between 1572 and 1645, still reminds us of Venetian power.

1. View the sea walls and the harbour from the sea end of the car park (page 52).
2. Walk along the quay to the New Fort, which stands high over the harbour, and see the Lion Door of the original main entrance to the fort (page 53).
3. Continue inland with the New Fort on your right, through the recently restored square and right into Solomos Street, past the domed church and the entrance to the New Fort on the right and up the stairs through a tunnel in the walls of the New Fort into the market (page 53). The market is being rebuilt. San Rocco (page 54) is the area to the west of San Rocco Square, the traffic hub of the new town, two hundred metres further on from the market.

The Old Port in 1961, when Theresa Nicholas arrived in Corfu.

HARBOUR 1961

The fine caique 'St. Nicholas'!

ST NICHOLAS

Lion Door of the main entrance to the New Fort.

The market.

conversation
Greek style

THE EGG LADY.

THE MARKET

Donkey Saddle maker
San Rocco

Wine shops San Rocco

To the smart end of town . . .

This short walk starts in the middle of Nikiforou Theotoki Street. Go to the left of the tobacconist into M. Theotoki.

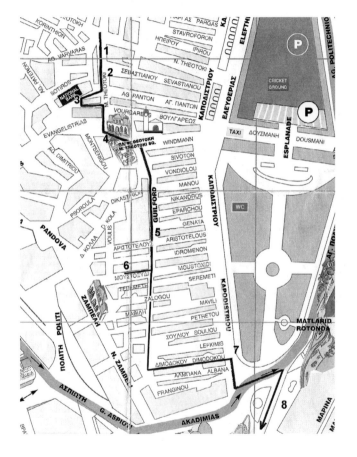

1. This was Vegetable Street in the 1960s. The only vegetable you can buy there today is the spinach in *spanakopita,* the pie taken out of the oven in the shop at the start of the street on the right.
2. On the left look at Sevastianou Street (page 56 left) and Ag. Panton Street (page 56 right) and then turn right into the square with the replica of a medieval cistern in the centre.
3. In the square at the end of the main shopping street, G. Theotoki Street, with the National Bank at one's back, look up to the campanile of the old Catholic Church of the 'Annunciata' Evangalistra (page 28).
4. Turn left down Evveniou Voulgareos Street and second right into the exquisite 17thC Town Hall Square, where the people of the town congregated in Venetian times and eat leisurely under canopies today. The Town Hall is made of stone from Sinies in the north-east of the island. Ahead is the 17thC Catholic Cathedral. At the top of the square is the Bank of Greece.
5. Stroll up Guilford Street past No. 59 (page 29).
6. Turn right into the narrow non-pedestrianised street, Moustoxidi. On your right is the old Pensione Suisse Hotel (page 57), where the Durrell family stayed when they first arrived on the island in the 1930s. R eturn to Guilford Street and go to the end.
7. Turn left down Dimodokou Street to the Esplanade and visit the bar on the roof of the beautiful old Cavalieri Hotel with its incredible view over the Esplanade and the Old Fort.
8. The energetic can continue round Garitsa Bay, to the south of the Old Fort, to the Windmill and sample the fish platter at Nautilus and then on to Mon Repos, the summer palace of the Greek royal family, and back via the ruins of Palaiopolis, the original settlement on the island, which includes the biggest Roman *agora* in the Mediterranean.

Sevastianou Street.

No. 32 Panton Street from under the arch in front of No. 27.

THE SCULPTURES ON THE OLD PENSIONE SWISS MOUSTOXIDE St.

Old Pensione Suisse Hotel – the Durrell family stayed here in the 1930s, when they first arrived on the island.

Easter . . .

To the visitor from the West, with its commercialised Christmas as the high point of the church year, Orthodox Easter is an eye-opener. At the end of Lent, during Holy Week and Easter Week, the Greeks celebrate the Resurrection. The island welcomes tens of thousands of visitors from Athens and the mainland.

On Palm Sunday the body of St. Spiridon, accompanied by the island's philharmonic bands, is taken around the old town walls to commemorate the deliverance from the plague in 1630. Holy Week continues with church services on every day.

Good Friday is the day for the *Epitaphios*, the funeral procession of Christ. Sketches on pages 30 to 32 vividly portray the occasion when the churches parade their funeral biers around the town. The first *Epitaphios* leaves the church in the New Fort at two in the afternoon; the last from the Orthodox Cathedral at ten in the evening. The Philharmonics again march, now playing sombre music including Albinoni's *Adagio*, Verdi's *Marcia Funebre* and Chopin's *Funeral March*.

Holy Saturday starts at nine in the morning with the procession of St. Spiridon including the *Epitaphios* of the Church of Agios Spiridon. Music includes Faccio's *Hamlet* and Beethoven's *Funeral March*. At 11 o'clock, with the Liston and the west side of the Esplanade crowded to bursting point, huge pots are thrown out from windows above. This tradition goes back, perhaps, to the Venetians who threw out old crockery on January 1st, or to early Christian times as an act of stoning Judas or even to pagan times. Villages across the island now repeat this ceremony.

The evening ends with a midnight mass around the bandstand on the Esplanade to celebrate the Anastasi, *Xristo anesti*, Christ has arisen, followed by an enormous firework display on the Old Fort. Finally, everyone goes off to a taverna to celebrate the ending of Lent.

Early on Easter Sunday, churches in town have further parades and then the island sits down to eat spit-roasted lambs.

On Easter Monday, each village has its own parade with the churches bringing out their cross and standard. New Week continues with parades on each day somewhere on the island. During Easter Week, hard-boiled eggs which have been dyed red are knocked together sharp end against sharp end.

Corfu

The villages

"The beauty of the villages here is something not to be described – for no place in the world is so lovely, I think. The whole island is in undulations from the plain where the city is, to the higher hills on the west side; and all the space is covered with one immense grove of olive trees, so that you see over a carpet of wood wherever you look."

Edward Lear, The Corfu Years 13 December 1855

Corfu – the villages

Corfu, above all, is a green paradise. Covered in olive trees, with cypresses standing tall and slender, the island hides its ultimate secret: its villages.

The modern tourist, driving along the main roads around the island, can be forgiven for seeing few of its 104 villages. Development these days is along the coast; the wild western beaches and the coves of the north-east are glorious.

So where are all the villages?

This pertinent question was also asked by previous invaders: the pirates that roamed the Mediterranean in years gone by. The cunning Corfiots' simple solution was to move inland and onto high ground, which had a further advantage: it was away from the marshes where mosquitoes bred. To the Venetian arrival and their demand for cheap oil for the lamps of Venice, the villagers' response was to plant three million olive trees. Many of these ancient trees can still be found.

The island is today faced by new invaders.

At Easter, tens of thousands of Greeks from Athens, Thessaloniki and the towns on the mainland arrive in Corfu. In the summer, hundreds of thousands of foreigners from Britain, Germany and the countries of the north fly in. They sit in their favourite tavernas; they talk; they drink; they dream: of the place they will one day buy on the island to escape from the hot, humid Greek summers or the cold, wet northern winters.

The Greeks will buy in Corfu Town and then perhaps in the villages, where there are still beautiful old houses to restore. The foreigners prefer to buy their Mediterranean villa in the olive groves. I hope this book will make the latter think again and consider restoring a village house. They will then become part of the island community.

The map on the right shows the 30 villages where Theresa Nicholas has sketched. Many other beautiful ones exist, particularly in the mainly agricultural area of Lefkimmi, the southern Angevin region of the island. Messis, the area in the centre of the island, has probably the most vibrant villages; they are near Corfu Town and ideal for all-year-round living. Those in the north are more likely to be set in the mountains and some of them are derelict.

In style, Corfu villages are fairly similar: a central square, *plateia*; a church with a beautiful bell-tower; and narrow alleyways seen through ornate arches. Theresa's sketches bring out their remarkable architecture. At the end of the book you will find how she has captured on paper thirty years of village life – a true climax to an inspiring collection.

Choose your villages

Village	Region	Pages
Ag Markos *	Oros	100, 101
Ag Prokopios	Messis	81, 65
Ag Theodora	Messis	81, 66, 84
Ano Garouna	Messis	81, 83
Ano Korakiana *	Oros	100, 72
Armenades	Gyro	95, 67, 96
Avliotes	Gyro	95, 97
Daphnata	Messis	81, 85
Gardelades	Gyro	95, 68, 97
Gastouri	Messis	81, 69, 86, 87
Giannades	Messis	81, 88
Horepiskopi	Gyro	95, 70, 98
Kalafationes	Messis	81, 79
Kamara	Messis	81, 89
Kastellani Messis	Messis	81, 90
Kato Garouna	Messis	81, 71
Kavadades	Gyro	95, 99
Kavallouri	Gyro	95, 98
Klimatia	Oros	100, 102
Kouramades	Messis	81, 73
Lakones	Gyro	95, 78
Liapades	Gyro	95, 74, 79, 97
Makrades	Gyro	95, 99
Nymphes	Oros	100, 101
Pelekas	Messis	81, 78, 90, 91
Perithia	Oros	100, 103
Potomos	Messis	81, 75, 92
Sinarades	Messis	81, 76, 93
Skripero	Oros	100, 77, 104
Varipatades	Messis	81, 94

* Historically in Messis
Spelling may vary on sketches

AG. PROKOPIS

AY. THEODORA

1780

GARDELADES

GASTOURI

ITYRESPIKOPI

KATa GAiROUNa

Korikiana.

KOORACIADES

LiAPADes

Potamos

SINARADES   Pale greens

SKRIPERO

THERESA NICHOLAS

1803   LAKONES

PELEKAS

LIAPADES

KALAFATIONES

PROS LAKONES
FOOT PATH FROM
PALEOKASTRITZA

The Messis – the centre of the island

Agios Prokopios, set in the depths of the countryside of Central Corfu, is one of the region's most picturesque villages, with narrow lanes winding up to a hilltop church. Edward Lear described it as: "This beautiful place: the quiet warmth and semi-shade are delightful."

Agia Theodora is a charming neighbourhood of Agios Prokopios.

Ano Garouna sprawls across the western flanks of Mount Agii Deka, and enjoys spectacular sea views. "I walked to Garouna where there is a beautiful view of the Citadel and city and the channel," wrote Edward Lear.

Daphnata, set high above Benitses at a major crossing point on the main east-central mountain ridge, enjoys spectacular views both over the sea to Corfu Town and inland. It forms one of half a dozen hamlets that make up the larger traditional settlement of Stavros.

Gastouri, set on the inland slopes of a ridge, looks out westward across a fertile valley. The village consists of numerous small neighbourhoods linked by little lanes and footpaths. It is home of the Achillion Palace, built for the Empress Elizabeth of Austria in 1890, and its philharmonic orchestra, founded in 1898, was the first to be established out of Town. "The view from the Benitses Road is one of the loveliest on the island," wrote Edward Lear.

Giannades stands on the lower slopes of the line of hills which border the western fringe of the Ropa Valley, Corfu's most extensive inland plain. Agricultural in origin, the village has been greatly upgraded recently, and the view from its delightful square over the Valley is not to be missed.

Kalafationes is a hill-top village amongst glorious olive groves which, in 2002, were badly burnt in a fire which seriously damaged a magnificent mansion with its fine library.

Kamara, tucked under the looming bulk of Mount Agii Deka and drenched in greenery, has a well with excellent water. A partly restored small monastery, dedicated to Agios Vlassis and featuring Byzantine wall frescoes, is a short walk from the village centre.

Kastellani Messis was capital of the Messis (central) region until 1912, but is now a backwater. It is set in an open position and has an extensive square, and is famous for its fiesta, which Lawrence Durrell describes in 'Prospero's Cell'.

Kato Garouna occupies an amphitheatre with its back to a huge hill and faces Ano Garouna across a deep valley. The village is extensive and full of well-built houses featuring the traditional local architecture and local stone.

Kouramades is one of Corfu's most picturesque and well-kept villages, with a narrow main street bordered by typical old houses. It centres around a square with three well-heads. Next to the attractive church is an old barber's shop, still functioning after nearly 60 years.

Pelekas is a hilltop village on the west coast, most famous for the 'Kaiser's Throne,' a fabulous viewpoint where Kaiser Wilhelm II would watch the sun go down over the sea. The village is unique in that it has embraced tourism without damaging its picturesque character.

Potamos, though now a suburb of Corfu Town, remains traditional in style. The long, narrow main street is bordered on both sides with picturesque arcades. "Potamos, with its clean and straw-hatted gray-trousered men, and its velvet-pelissed yellow-hooded respectable lovely women," wrote Edward Lear.

Sinarades, set on a sweeping hill and facing inland, is a large village with well-preserved Venetian buildings, two fine campaniles and a Folk Museum dedicated to preserving the traditions of Central Corfu. The village has a philharmonic orchestra which was founded in 1960. On the outskirts of the village, Aerostato boasts a famous view over Agios Gordis beach.

Varipatades is located on a low ridge in the centre of the island and contains the most convoluted network of lanes and alleys of any village in Corfu. It has many traditional houses featuring the local architectural style.

ANO GAROUNA

ANO GAROUNA

Ag Theodora

Daphnateri 1851

GASTOURI

GASTOURI

GASTOURI

GASTOURI

GIANNADES

GIANNADES

– 88 –

KAMARA

KAMARA

KASTELLANI MESSIS

Pelekas

PELEKAS.

PELEKAS

Potamos

SINARADES

VARIPATATHES

VARIPATADES '83

The Gyro – the north-west of the island

Armenades, a small village in north-west Corfu, was first settled by refugees from Armenia. Its population is mainly occupied in cultivating the rich fields of the valley and hillsides which surround it.

Avliotes runs along one of the weathered sandstone ridges which cross north-west Corfu. The village has a thriving population and is renowned for the lively traditional coffee shops that cluster around the village square.

Gardelades sits on the southern end of a shallow flat-topped cone, surrounded on almost three sides by plains. It boasts many fine mansion-style houses with traditional architectural features.

Horepiskopi, bypassed by the main road north, is quiet and traditional. "Hokus Pokus, as the English call it, is on a double rocky hill in the midst of a valley entirely full of splendid oranges and cypresses," said Edward Lear.

Kavadades is a sprawling settlement which includes a number of outlying hamlets, all set on a rolling plateau in north-west Corfu. It is a down-to-earth farming community, not particularly

pretty but with easy access to three of Corfu's best beaches.

Kavallouri extends along one of the long sandstone ridges which run from east to west across the north-west of Corfu. The village has views in both directions over lush valleys, and is characterised by the numerous substantial mansions which border its single main street.

Lakones, settled in the Medieval period by refugees from Lakonia, is one of the few Corfu villages with a sea view; indeed, nearby 'Bella Vista' claims the best view in the Mediterranean. The village is set high above the sea and has narrow, immensely picturesque streets and alleys.

Liapades is famous for its extensive village square, which is dominated by a lovely old church and is surrounded by coffee bars where visitors can try the local *kakotrygis*, 'hard-to-pick', wine. A maze of narrow alleys extends from the square, with many fine mansions and arched doorways to be admired.

Makrades is located high above the coast near Paleokastritsa, and close to the Medieval fortress of Angelokastro. The village, a huddle of stone houses, many deserted, tumbles down a rocky hillside with extensive sea and mountain views.

ARMENADES

AVLIOTES

GARDELADES

Gardelades

LIAPADES

Well Horepikopi

KAVALLOURI

SAMUELLI HOUSE   KAVADADES

MAICRADES

The Oros – the north-east of the island

Agios Markos, one of two on Corfu designated as a 'heritage village', has maintained its style and atmosphere. It is built on the lower slopes of the great 'wall' which defines the southern side of the Pantokrator Massif, and looks out over the Bay of Ipsos. Most of its population was relocated following a landslide in the 1960s. The Church of Agios Merkourios has frescoes dating from 1075.

Ano Korakiana is a very large village set on the steep slopes of Pantokrator's southern 'wall'. With a population of 1400 and many traditional buildings, it has 37 churches and a musical tradition going back to 1623, when the Mantolinatas of the Pope were founded.

Klimatia is one of several villages which dot a little-visited plateau in Corfu's unspoiled central north. The village has an open aspect and is close to many pure mountain springs.

Nymphes, in ancient times, was called 'The Place of the Nereids' (water nymphs) and its name still hints of the powerful streams which have carved out the hidden valleys of its hinterland. Close to the village is the Askitario, an ancient and very picturesque monastery, now abandoned.

Perithia was first occupied in the Byzantine era, when frequent pirate raids drove the population away from the comfortable coast to a harsher life in the mountains. Most of the mainly ruined houses of Old Perithia date from the 16th–18th centuries. The village is set in a great bowl under the shadow of Mount Pantokrator's cone-shaped summit, and is in the process of being restored. It has nine churches and four tavernas.

Skripero is a large village which extends over the lower slopes of the southern wall of the Pantokrator Massif and down onto the plain at its foot. It used to be the administrative capital of a long-defunct municipality, and contains many fine mansions.

AG. MARKOS

NYMPHES

KLIMATIA

Skrupero

CORBELS

Village life . . .

The Dog →

At home . . .

HOREPISKOPI

Girls in Festive Costume

Barrels . . .

HOREPISKOPI

. . . and urns

In church

At work

Treading the grapes

Washing the barrels

Chickens . . .

. . . and goats

PROS KATAVOLOS   24.2.96

Picking the olives

Pressing the olives

PELEKAS.

Packing up

Going home

YIANNIS BOOKS

John Waller trained as an engineer, founded a computer company and invented software. He was a Liberal councillor in Richmond for 17 years and three times parliamentary candidate for Twickenham.

For his sixtieth birthday, he cooked his friends a thirteen course Greek dinner and they gave him a punt, which started his writing. **Three Persons in a Punt** will be published when he has finished his journey from source to sea down the Thames.

He sent his first book, **Greek Walls**, to 99 agents. 98 said "No"; one said "Self-publish" and Yiannis Books was born.

Other books published by Yiannis Books are:

2004   **Greek Walls – an Odyssey in Corfu** by John Waller
2005   **Corfu Sunset – Avrio never comes** by John Waller
2006   **Irish Flames – Peter Waller's true story of the Black and Tans** by John Waller
2007   **The Papas and the Englishman – from Corfu to Zagoria** by Roy Hounsell, introduced by John Waller

In 2007, John wrote the play of the book, **Irish Flames**, which was rehearse-read at the Irish Centre in Hammersmith. He is looking for a theatre to put the play on.

"We were interested to read the adaptation, which is assuredly written. The play offers a powerful comment on wartime violence and retribution." *Royal Court*

"My play should strike a cord with those concerned about our presence in Iraq and Afghanistan." *John Waller*

Details are on www.yiannisbooks.com.

John Waller, engineer and ex-politician, when given a punt for his 60th birthday, started his writing journey:
2004 *Greek Walls*
2005 *Corfu Sunset*
2006 His first novel
200? *3 persons in a punt*
(From source to sea down the Thames!)

You've been to Greece? "Wallow in nostalgia" with *Greek Walls*
You've never been to Corfu? Read *Greek Walls* and you'll go!

In 1966, John Waller and his Danish wife fall in love with Corfu, 'a heaven on earth'. On the wild west coast, they build a small summer house, which nearly slides down the mountain. Their neighbour pumps sewage onto their land …

"Often funny, always informative"
Hilary Whitton Paipeti, The Corfiot

"Most enjoyable read"
Lesley Toll, Daily Mail

"Wildly entertaining"
Tom Teodorczuk, Evening Standard

yiannisbooks@aol.com

Front cover 'View from the villa' by kesselerob@aol.com

UK   £7.99
EU   12 euro
US $15

ISBN 0-9547887-0-2

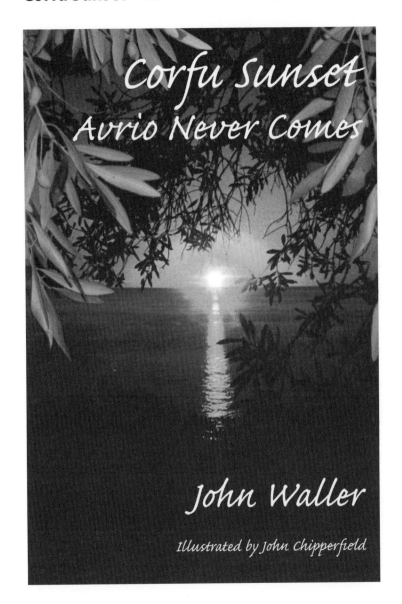

Corfu Sunset
Avrio Never Comes

John Waller

Illustrated by John Chipperfield

John Waller, engineer and ex-politician, when given a punt for his 60th birthday, started his writing journey:
2004 *Greek Walls*
2005 *Corfu Sunset*
2006 His first novel
200? *3 persons in a*

You love Greece? How about the Greek workmen?
Fancy living in the sun? Read *Corfu Sunset* first

Just retired John Waller and his Danish wife decide to renovate their near-derelict holiday home. They gain control from their neighbour who has pumped sewage on their land.

In a frenetic summer they build a road up the mountain and a pool, veranda and new roof for their villa. A party is held to celebrate a great Greek victory.

Delightful episodes and characters emerge from the pages of *Corfu Sunset*. A highly amusing account of the highs and lows of property ownership abroad with attention to detail that puts most travel authors in the shade.
Tom Teodorczuk, **Evening Standard**

Corfu Sunset is essential reading for anyone thinking of moving abroad to a place in the sun, revealing with panache and passion the rewards and drawbacks of buying property in a remote but warm outpost of southern Europe.
Nigel Lewis, **Daily Mail**

yiannisbooks@aol.com

Front cover by Helena Hutchinson
'Sunset through the olive tree'.

ISBN 0-9547887-1-0

9 780954 788711 >

UK	£7.99
EU	Euro 12
US	$15

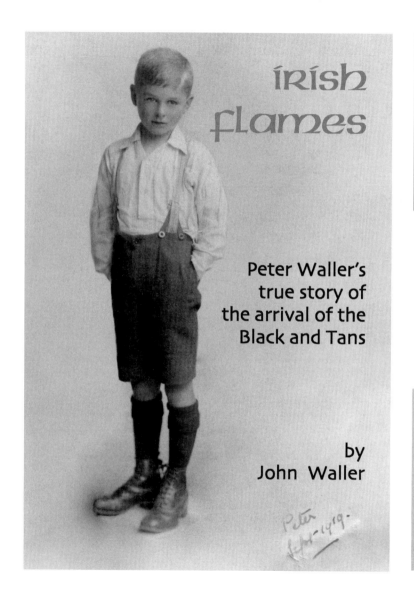

irish
flames

Peter Waller's
true story of
the arrival of the
Black and Tans

by
John Waller

Before Peter Waller died – he is pictured on the front cover aged eight – he gave a partial manuscript to the author, his half-brother. Here is Peter's story.

"IRELAND in 1920. The Black and Tans have just arrived to crush the growing Irish Revolution and one boy watches as his country is torn apart by flames of freedom, hate and love.

Irish Flames is a thriller based on the intimate memories of Peter Waller – a boy growing up during those troubled times.

Stories of the brutality of The Black and Tans have been passed down through generations of families but now the words of an eyewitness can show us what it was really like.

Anybody with even a little Irish blood in his or her veins will find this story a remarkable account of the end of British Rule."

The Irish Post (April 22)

ISBN 0954788729

£8.99 €12.99

www.yiannisbooks.com

ISBN 0-9547887-2-9

9 780954 788728

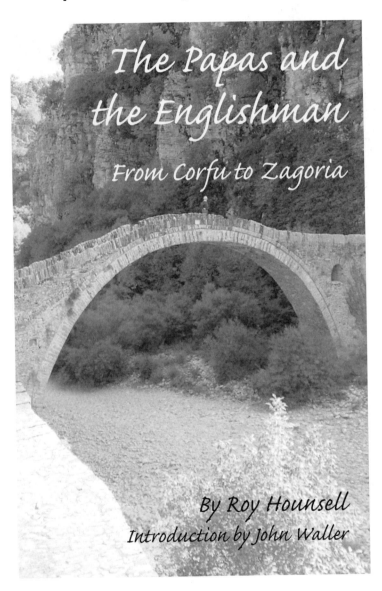

The Papas and
the Englishman

From Corfu to Zagoria

By Roy Hounsell

Introduction by John Waller

In 1991 Patrick Leigh Fermor was asked, "If you wanted to go somewhere – somewhere right off the map, with no tourists or modern developments – where would you go?"

He replied: "Epirus – the north, the mountains. You might have a chance of finding places there." It was in 1991 that Roy and Effie Hounsell moved into their place in Zagoria.

In 1980, having been made redundant, Roy and his wife left England to try their hand at establishing themselves in Corfu. They visited mountainous Zagoria in Northern Mainland Greece and were captivated by its magnificent, rugged beauty and its mouldering, unspoiled stone villages. All desire to move there was dashed by their poor ability to speak Greek. Eventually they bought a tumble-down property in Koukouli. They struggled with the rebuilding, helped by the village priest, Papa Kostas, created a garden out of the jungle and joined in with the villagers to become regarded as locals.

"What makes this different from other "No Going Back" sagas is how the authors have engaged with their neighbours and helped keep an isolated community alive." *Marc Dubin, co-author, Rough Guide to Greece*

"Charting the progress of the author's transformation from 'outsider' into genuine local, this book sets standards for the relocation genre. Roy Hounsell writes lovingly about the beautiful location, and unpatronizingly about the people he meets and befriends along the way." *Hilary Whitton-Paipeti, Editor, The Corfiot*

"Many of us dream of buying and renovating a house in the mountains – but Roy Hounsell's unusual tale of his Greek adventure is a useful and well-paced read." *Nigel Lewis, Managing. Editor, A Place in the Sun Magazine*

yiannisbooks@aol.com

UK   £ 7.99
EU   Euro 12
US $ 15

ISBN 978-0-9547887-3-5

9 780954 788735 >